Rainbows in the Snow

Rainbows in the Snow

A celebration of life's journeys and discoveries through words and photos

Cheryl Landes

Tabby Cat Communications

Rainbows in the Snow © Cheryl Landes, 2024

Rainbows in the Snow is a work of nonfiction and fiction. In the nonfiction pieces, the names and identifying details of certain individuals have been changed to protect their privacy. For the works of fiction, the names, characters, organizations, places, events, and incidents are either products of the author's imagination or are used fictitiously. Any resemblances to any actual persons, living or dead, or actual events are purely coincidental.

All rights reserved. No part of this book may be reproduced, stored in a retrieval system, or transmitted in any form or by any means without the advanced written permission of the publisher, except by a reviewer who may quote brief passages in a review to be published in a newspaper, magazine, journal, or online.

Published in the United States by Tabby Cat Communications, Camas, WA
Cover design and book layout by HR Hegnauer
Tabby Cat Communications logo design by Charlie Okada
Photographs by Cheryl Landes
ISBN 979-8-9895450-0-1, paperback
ISBN 979-8-9895450-1-8, ebook

Table of Contents

- 1   Welcome to Rainbows in the Snow
- 5   Sunrise
- 10   An Attack Cat in Montana
- 14   A Chocolate Chip Cookie Romance in 89 Words
- 15   A Cobblestone Christmas Eve
- 17   A Freeway Tweet
- 18   A Letter to a Song
- 20   A Reason to Live
- 24   An Encounter with a Seal
- 26   Bernadette
- 29   Dreams and Realities
- 35   Eugene
- 40   If You were Here
- 41   Kiku's Masterpiece
- 44   Kisses
- 46   Life Cycles
- 48   Mockingbird
- 49   My Favorite Road Sign
- 50   Nurselogs
- 54   Perfectly Imperfect
- 56   Sea Lion Zen
- 57   Seeing through the Storm

59	Shopping for Pants at a French Market
64	Slow Ride
67	Spring Haiku
69	The Bird Emergency
73	The Boy at the Market
77	The Face in the Rock
79	The Building Inspector
89	The Feline Arbitrator
92	The Ghost of Golden
97	The Girl on the Ferry
99	The Positive Side of Addiction
102	Trailheads
107	Who's that Hottie?
111	Sunsets
117	Acknowledgments

Welcome to Rainbows in the Snow

Snowshoeing is my winter hiking. When I lived in Massachusetts from 2001 until 2006, I often snowshoed in Wachusett Meadow Wildlife Sanctuary, a Mass Audubon property in Princeton. I rarely saw anyone wandering these quiet, snow-covered hills and meadows with beaver lodges scattered along the shores of the frozen ponds. I never saw any beavers there, though there was plenty of evidence of their presence left behind in tree trunks half nibbled or sawed through by their sharp teeth.

Along this trail, the sun's rays often reflected in the ice crystals. When the angle was just right, little prisms of rainbows projected in the ice. I loved seeing them but could never capture them on camera.

These tiny gifts inspired the title for this book. My goal is to celebrate journeys by sharing stories about the transformations, realizations, discoveries, and resolutions along the way. I hope you enjoy these stories and photos as much as I enjoyed creating them for you.

To making many rainbows,
Cheryl

A snow-covered trail at Wachusett Meadow
Wildlife Sanctuary in Princeton, Massachusetts

Beaver lodge in Wachusett Meadow Wildlife Sanctuary

A tree trunk partially cut by beavers' teeth
in Wachusett Meadow Wildlife Sanctuary

Sunrise

Early this morning, I sit on the bed at a guest house in Laugarvatn, Iceland, and watch tiny, low white clouds slice through the late October darkness. Higher in the sky above the west end of the lake, a giant blob glows like molten lava. The ragged orb doesn't reflect in the lake. If I hadn't arrived here before sunset today, I wouldn't know the lake exists because it blends into the darkness. I can't see the source of the light. I ask whether it's intentional, and the radiance intensifies. Maybe I don't need an answer. I will savor this magical moment, be grateful I'm here, and greet the sun in three hours, when it will push the clouds away and guide me on a new adventure.

Another morning in late September, I wanted to watch the sun rise over the Atlantic Ocean but didn't know where to go, so I rose in the darkness and drove more than an hour from central Massachusetts to southern Maine, then exited the interstate and followed Route 1 through coastal towns, chasing signs to popular viewpoints, lighthouses, and beaches. Although the scenery in the early dawn light was beautiful, nothing spoke to me. I wasn't sure what I was looking for until ten minutes later, when I parked at a small beach near a wildlife sanctuary. The red-orange sky reflected on the waves and sand, and grass resembling wheat danced in the wind, celebrating the arrival of a new day. I joined them.

Another morning in early-September, I stood in the dew-laden grass at Dancing Spirit Ranch in Montana and watched

Sunrise in Laugarvatn, Iceland

Sunrise reflections in Hot Lake near La Grande, Oregon

the sunrise. The rays cast gold in the ripples in the small lake in front of me and on a wooden canoe tied to a weathered dock. A pair of paddles waited inside the canoe, beckoning me to row to the other side, but I didn't accept the offer. Despite standing near the shore in soaked shoes and socks, I wanted to enjoy this peaceful scene as long as it lasted.

Another morning in early October, steam rose from Hot Lake in northeastern Oregon, generating fog in the nippy air. I stood behind the cattails, watching the sun rise slowly as it tried to break through the clouds and reflect on the lake. A flock of ducks and a goose glided near the edge of the lake opposite the geothermal springs. I wanted to stay here longer but it was time to go home.

On mornings when the rain sleeps on the west side of Oregon and Washington, the black silhouette of Mount Hood appears in front of a yellow, orange, red, and purple layered canvas. The sapphire water in the Columbia River flows from the bottom of the painting to my vantage point in Vancouver, Washington. These sunrises are always a treat after long stretches of cloudy, misty days that nourish the earth and among the many reasons I call this beautiful place home.

Sunrise near Biddeford, Maine

Sunrise at Dancing Spirit Ranch in Columbia Falls, Montana

An Attack Cat in Montana

During a driving trip through southern Montana, my mother and I stopped for a break in the town of Big Timber. We passed Country Crossroads, a shop with an eclectic mix of items for sale outside: water fountains, windmills, a bird feeder, a lamp post shaped like a T with an elk on top, an old Coca-Cola sign, pinwheels, brown stars, and metal black-eyed Susans. After a quick lunch and filling up the car with gas, we returned to browse on our way back to the interstate.

When we walked to the entrance, I saw a sign at the bottom of the glass door that read, "Warning: Attack cat."

What would an attack cat do? I wondered. Would it jump on me and dig into my back with its claws? Would it growl and hiss at me while chasing me around the store? Would it tackle my ankles and knock me down, then lock me up and demand a case of its favorite treats in exchange for my release? Or would it try to rub me into submission, whatever that may be?

Mom and I stepped inside. Inches ahead of us, a brown Maine coon with black stripes sat next to some wooden boxes with drawers and its big green eyes stared at us. It strolled over to me and began rubbing my shoes and ankles.

The shopkeeper on duty appeared and said, "Hello." She looked at the cat, then back at me.

"Is this the attack cat?" I asked.

The shopkeeper chuckled. "This is Freddie. He's harmless."

"Is it okay if I pet him?"

She smiled. "Sure. He'll love it."

Country Crossroads in Big Timber, Montana

Freddie, the attack cat in Montana

I squatted and rubbed Freddie between the ears for a few seconds. I could feel him purring as he soaked in my strokes and the sensations from rubbing my ankles. Then he followed Mom and me to the counter, stopped in front of my feet, and looked up at me with wide eyes begging for more attention. I squatted again and rubbed his head and back. Soon he rolled on his back and spread his legs like an upside-down flying squirrel—an invitation to rub his stomach.

I'm always reluctant to rub cats' tummies because often they curl like a grubworm and grab my hand with claws extended on all four paws and won't let go. But I decided to take a chance with Freddie. When I first touched him, he spread his legs wider as if he was saying, "That's the spot! More!" He squeezed his eyes shut and the more I rubbed him, the louder he purred.

The shopkeeper and Mom watched, smiling the entire minute Freddie let me rub him. Then he rolled over, rose, stretched in a downward dog yoga pose, and sauntered into a room behind the counter.

Mom and I started shopping. We browsed aisles packed with random items grouped in an organizational pattern that made sense to only whoever arranged them. There was a little bit of everything, from place settings to dolls, nails to bridles for horses, and even a nook filled with gently-used Christmas ornaments. Mom bought a pair of earrings from a small display on the counter.

I expected to see Freddie again, but he didn't return. Probably he was napping in that back room, replenishing his energy to attack his next victim.

A Chocolate Chip Cookie Romance in 89 Words

I baked a batch of chocolate chip cookies to share with my roommate. Then I thought about the man I dated twice, two doors down. He likes chocolate. I filled a bag and left it outside his door with a note, "Enjoy, Cheryl." Then I worried. Am I being too forward? I really like this guy. A few hours later, he knocked on my door. I answered, saw his beaming face and twinkling hazel eyes, and heard his heartfelt, "Thank you. They were delicious!" We married four years later.

A Cobblestone Christmas Eve

I met Belle while eating lunch in the student union during my junior year in college. She was a soft-spoken woman with short black curly hair and creamy skin, probably ten years older than me.

She sat at my table and we began chatting, which became a daily routine I looked forward to. Two weeks later, she asked, "Are you going home for Christmas?"

"No," I said. "My family is too far away."

"Would you like to celebrate Christmas Eve at my place?"

I accepted. Then she said, "Bring something for a gift swap—something you already have. Don't buy anything."

That night, we chatted for hours in front of her Christmas tree, drank cider, munched on sugar cookies, and swapped gifts. I gave her an unused writing journal I found in the closest. She gave me a cobblestone from Portugal, where she spent most of her life. She spoke passionately about her experiences there. I sensed she was homesick but felt honored to hear her stories.

Belle transferred to another college spring term and we lost contact, but I still have the cobblestone in my treasure box. Every time I look at it, I think of that special holiday.

Icy patterns on a sandbar in the Nooksak River
in northwestern Washington

A Freeway Tweet

The driver of the Corvette tailed me on the 25-mph exit ramp to the interstate. I pulled over to let him race past me. Less than a quarter mile later, a wall of traffic stopped him. #karma

Nap time at the Hemingway House in Havana, Cuba

A Letter to a Song

Dear "You Raise Me Up,"

   For the past month, I hear you on Magic 106.7, the pop radio station in Boston, every time I leave the Family to Family class and mental health support group at the Unitarian church in Bedford. You start singing to me as soon as I turn onto the road from Bedford to Concord.

   Is this a coincidence? Do you know how drained I am from struggling with my husband's mental illness? We're apart now, and I don't know where he is. I'm forced to file for divorce to protect myself financially while I struggle to pay the mounting debt. When our marriage began falling apart, that's when I learned how bad our finances really are.

   You urge me to come and spend a while with you. You want to raise me up to climb mountains and walk on stormy seas. You say I'm strong when I'm on your shoulders, and when you raise me up, I can be more than I believe. It's hard for me to believe this most of the time, but the more I hear you, your truth slowly seeps in.

   You bring me comfort every time I hear you. You encourage me. You give me hope. I long to hear you every time I turn on the radio. Please, never stop singing to me and the other downtrodden people who need to hear your beautiful, inspirational message. We need you more than you'll ever know. Or maybe you do, and that's why you come.

Thank you,
Cheryl

Flower bed in Winlock, Washington

"You Raise Me Up" was composed by Rolf Løvland and written by Brendan Graham. The song was first recorded by Secret Garden on the album, *Once in a Red Moon*, which was released in December 2001. Other artists have recorded the song since then, including Josh Groban on his *Closer* album in September 2004. Groban's version of the recording became a major hit.

A Reason to Live

"Write about a reason to live," says Jennifer, our flash fiction workshop instructor. "You have ten minutes."

Write about only one reason to live? I ask myself. There are too many to choose from, so I make a list instead:

- Admiring the power and beauty of waterfalls
- Long walks in the rain listening to the drops tapping on the umbrella above my head
- Long walks on the beach
- Sitting on a driftwood log watching the sun's light paint red, orange, and purple swatches across the sky as it slides into the ocean
- Following a trail through the woods to see where it ends
- Following another trail to the top of a mountain to soak in the view
- Strolling through a garden filled with flowers in full bloom
- Playing fetch with a dog
- Flying in a hot air balloon
- Reading good books
- Listening to my favorite music, which changes depending on my mood
- Cuddling with the cats at an animal shelter or cat café
- Hugging an alpaca
- Laughing at an otter's antics

Rainbow at Skógafoss Falls in Iceland

- Watching the bald eagles during the winter migration
- Watching the sandhill cranes and snow geese during the spring migration
- Watching wildlife anywhere at any time
- Hiking with friends, with or without their dogs
- Breathing in the fragrance of lilacs in full bloom
- Kayaking on a peaceful lake
- Taking my mother on long drives along the Oregon Coast, her favorite
- Going on drives to find quirky stuff like the world's largest egg, the country's smallest post office, or the world's largest purple spoon
- Exploring ghost towns
- Hanging out just for the fun of it
- Admiring the popsicle colors of a rainbow after a summer shower

How many reasons to live can you write down in 10 minutes?

World's largest purple spoon in East Glacier, Montana

An Encounter with a Seal

My favorite summer adventure was my first visit to Lime Kiln Point State Park on San Juan Island, Washington. When I arrived, I followed the coastal trails in hopes of spotting the J Pod. Apparently I arrived too late, because the board in front of the lighthouse reported Orca sightings much earlier that day.

I decided to take some pictures of the views from the beach in hopes the whales would return. So I walked toward a spot near the water's edge, where I would wait.

But then something else stopped me a few yards from the shore. A seal pup was beached on the rocks just a few feet from the water. At first I didn't see it, because it blended well with the rocks. It stared at me, and I froze. It then looked away with reassurance that I would not harm it.

I kept still for an hour, watching it, and occasionally taking a picture or two. The seal glanced at me periodically but never seemed concerned. Likely it was under orders from its mother to stay there until she returned.

I left the park after that. I never saw any Orcas but was elated about my experience. I was also grateful for my grandparents' upbringing on how to react to animals in the wild: Be quiet and do not make any sudden moves to scare them. Because of that, I could enjoy a rare opportunity to observe a seal at close range in its natural habitat.

Originally published in the Washington State Parks newsletter, September 22, 2012

Lime Kiln Point State Park on San Juan Island, Washington

Seal pup at Lime Kiln Point State Park

Bernadette

One Sunday afternoon during a volunteer shift at Yoga with Cats at Animal Aid in Portland, I met a beautiful tabby with a white patch that reminded me of a bandana. Her name was Bernadette, according to the handwriting above her picture pinned to the bulletin board, and she was the lobby cat. When she saw me sit behind the front desk after class started, she jumped on the desk, laid next to my laptop, and stared at me with her big green eyes. Within minutes, she worked her way onto my lap and stayed there until the class ended.

Bernadette sat straight on my lap while I rubbed her head, ears, and back. She stared at me the entire time. I could hear and feel her purring. She was melting my heart, and she knew it. Oh, how I wanted to apply to adopt her and take her home, but I couldn't. I even told her so several times while we sat there, explained why I couldn't adopt her, and apologized. The more I apologized, the guiltier I felt. This girl wanted me to be her human.

I started volunteering at the shelter after my last cat died because I promised my mother, who lives with me, that I wouldn't adopt another one. The adjustments would have been too stressful for everyone involved.

When Yoga with Cats ended, I restored the classroom to its original condition and started to leave. Bernadette was on the counter in front of the desk, waiting for my return. I stopped to pet her one more time and fought the urge to fill out the paperwork. Finally, I tore myself away.

The next time I returned to the shelter, Bernadette wasn't there. Her picture was tacked to the new adoptions bulletin board hanging above the lobby desk. I smiled and silently wished her a long, happy life in her new home.

Bernadette at Animal Aid in Portland, Oregon

Dreams and Realities

1

I bit into the red grape, which oozed juice from its crunchy skin into my mouth and transported me to a cave filled with chocolate sauce. It wasn't hot fudge, my favorite topping for sundaes. No, it was milk chocolate, creamy and smooth. I didn't have anything against milk chocolate. Chocolate is chocolate, except when it's dark and hot, melting over a sundae, mingling its rich flavor into vanilla ice cream. My mouth watered from the thought, when I should have been concerned about a grape sending me to a strange place. I stepped into the brown pool and felt something grab my feet and pull me into the cool, sticky darkness. The deeper I sunk, I heard screams below me and wondered how anyone can scream, let alone talk, in this goo. Then I realized, I could still breathe. Where was this thing I couldn't see taking me?

2

Never race with a moose. They stress out easily and might jump in front of your car. If they do, you'll need to shop for a new car. But if you get lucky like I did that night, they'll run alongside your car for two miles at the park's speed limit of 20 miles per hour, then make a sharp right turn and disappear into the woods.

Bull moose in Ambejesus Lake at dusk near Millinocket, Maine

3

I'm running behind the school bus, yelling and waving at it to stop. I'm almost an arm's length away, but as soon as I catch up, it accelerates. No one sees me, except the eight-year-old girl with two auburn ponytails staring at me through the back door of the bus. She's so fascinated by my panic that she doesn't bother to tell anyone to stop for me. Or maybe she wants me to suffer.

4

Lulu, my friend's 90-pound Newfoundland, was an escape artist. One day, we strapped on her harness and started a walk in the neighborhood. The clerk at the pet store where my friend bought the harness yesterday said no dog had ever freed themselves from one. As we rounded a corner within three blocks of my friend's house, Lulu discovered a way to wiggle out of the harness. She ran a few yards, stopped until we were barely within arm's length of her, darted a few more yards, and repeated her game. Every time she turned around, she watched us through mischievous eyes and appeared to be smiling. "It's not funny," my friend said while we ran after her. Lulu responded by making a sharp left into a neighbor's yard and disappearing behind the house. My friend and I followed. When we entered the neighbor's backyard, Lulu was sitting under the patio table next to the homeowner, enjoying head rubs. Two guests sat on each side of the homeowner, enjoying drinks with him on this warm summer evening. We apologized for Lulu's intrusion, to which the homeowner replied, "No problem. We're dog people." He patted Lulu on the head again, then said, "She's such a sweet girl." Lulu looked at my friend and me with a cheesy grin on her face.

Lulu

5

Early one morning before the sun awoke, I walked on the shoulder of a gravel road, listening to the early morning chorus of crickets and bullfrogs. Steam rose from a pond ahead of me. Curious, I decided to get closer. I laid on the grass covered in heavy dew and rolled under the barbed wire fence. When I got up, I shivered from my wet clothes making contact with the chilly breeze. I walked to the shoreline, unlaced my shoes, and tossed them under a tree. After stepping into the warm mud, I paused to feel the goo ooze between my toes and cover my feet while the pond drew me in. Soon, a warm, peaceful feeling consumed me as I sunk to the bottom.

6

When you're running late for a flight, never pluck your cat from a windowsill and stuff her into a carrier when she's traveling with you. She will be quiet the entire ride to the airport, then stage a meltdown as soon as you arrive at the ticket counter. The agent will call a manager, who may or may not allow you on the plane. You'll spend some time convincing the manager that your cat is also a frequent flyer and she sleeps the entire flight. If your cat is Siamese, like my Misty was, her voice will echo off the walls of the airport, and everyone will express their sympathies to her by saying, "Poor kitty," through the security checkpoint while you want to hide under or behind anything in sight. After 45 minutes, she'll silence herself again, but by then, you've learned your lesson: You will never interrupt her squirrel watching again.

Misty

Eugene

When Eugene arrived at Animal Aid in Portland in 2017, he was a scrappy cat. At times, the brown tabby with a kinked tail was the friendliest kitty in the world. That's when he might roll around and play with me, or let me rub his head and between the ears. Sometimes when I rubbed him, he'd kiss my hand, which meant a soft lick or two. He loved lounging on a shelf on his favorite cat tree and watching the world go by.

But there were other times when he wasn't so sweet. Some days, he'd nip my hand if I tried to pet him. If I didn't heed his message, he'd bite me the next time. Other days, he'd growl or hiss at me if I came too close.

Every time I opened the shelter on Sunday for Yoga with Cats, my first task was to check on Eugene's demeanor. Then when the instructor and students checked in, I'd update them with either, "Eugene is in a good mood today," or "Eugene is having a bad day, so I advise staying away from him."

Gradually his charm and charisma began to shine through his rough edges as the caretakers and socializers worked with him. But when the COVID pandemic came in 2020 and he was still at the shelter, many of us wondered whether he would be a lifelong resident. I wanted to adopt him but couldn't because of my living situation.

There's a saying about two people being meant for each other, and this applies to animals and humans. Sometimes it takes time for the perfect matches to cross paths. Eugene's moment came when Susan Rooney found his profile while browsing the adoptions page on Animal Aid's website.

"The glamour shot on the website was very hard to resist," Susan said. "He had some special challenges that I knew I could meet if anyone could. I seemed to have the perfect setup for him, so I wanted to give him a cushy home. He has earned it."

Susan is a veteran of caring for many rescue cats, along with two purebred Maine coons, so she was ready for another challenge. She prefers adopting older males, because "they need homes more than kittens and even if that weren't the case, they have so much more personality than a kitten. It's a shame not to provide a home for them when you can."

Eugene arrived at Susan's home on September 1, 2020. When I asked her how Eugene was settling in during an interview for Animal Aid's newsletter, she said, "Things have been smoothing out a lot more quickly than I anticipated. I thought he might be a bit of a pain for a while until he got used to being here, but he's already turning into such a lover boy! I know that as time goes by, he will learn to trust me more and more and consequently become more relaxed, and we'll have even more fun!"

Speaking of fun, Eugene discovered a new toy after he settled in. "He's really big into rubber bands," Susan said. "The blue one is his favorite. I'm a little concerned he might swallow one, so I try to make sure he only has one at a time." He either carries his rubber band in his mouth while trotting through the house or leaves it in random spots for Susan to find.

Susan learned that Eugene liked to play fetch with the rubber band. "He had a hard time training me, but I finally figured it out. Now he brings me the rubber band, I snap it across the room, he finds it, brings it back, repeat."

It didn't take long for Susan to notice another side of Eugene. "He is quite emotionally intelligent and sensitive—even more than most cats," she said. "He'll jump up on the bed and look fixedly at me to see how I am feeling and might react. Or if I tell him to get off of something, he'll look at me first to see just how much trouble he is really in."

Susan is looking forward to the day when she and Eugene can snuggle. "I'm having a hard time being patient for it, but I know it is coming," she said. "I thought my last cat was the most affectionate cat in the world, but I think Eugene may give Eddie a run for his money in the affection department." Eddie, Susan's last cat, died six months before she adopted Eugene.

"I think Eugene is going to be a great companion."

Three years later, Eugene is still a work in progress, but he has come a long way. "He has become very affectionate, as long as I don't try to pick him up!" Susan said. "If I try to pick him up, all hell breaks loose. But otherwise, he's very sweet and well-behaved."

Eugene still keeps in contact with Animal Aid. He emails a Christmas card to the staff every year with a picture attached. In the latest message, he sat under a tree, staring at an ornament. Susan added this note at the bottom of the card: "Eugene wouldn't wear his costume this year."

Eugene

Heart-shaped rock near Bright Angel Lodge
in Grand Canyon National Park

If You were Here

You left four days before my fifteenth birthday. I found you on the floor lying unconscious on your left side, your body straddling the doorway connecting the living room and kitchen. A bruise was forming on your forehead, and a tube of Ben-Gay was open on the table beside you. You'd told me countless times that your arm was bothering you because your bursitis was flaring up, but when the coroner arrived at our farm, he said you died from a heart attack.

I was close to you, Grandma. You knew that. You encouraged and supported me through the happy and sad times. You noticed my love for school and urged me to get good grades so I could go to college, get a degree, and have a prosperous life. You finished high school, but Grandpa didn't. He never learned how to read because his formal education ended in the fourth grade. His mother, who lost her husband, needed help on the farm. In the 1800s, that's what kids did—they helped their parents. Family took priority over everything, even school.

Grandma, you were never ashamed of him. You read for him, behind closed doors, so we couldn't see what you were doing. But we knew. We never talked about it. Before he got sick and died four years before you, he'd had a successful blue-collar career. You were proud of him, always.

If you were here now, I would say "thank you" for your love and support. I never said it enough. Although you've been gone for almost fifty years, I know you're still watching over me, and I hope you're proud of me.

Kiku's Masterpiece

For this year's open house at Animal Aid, some of our cats who were ready for adoption created paintings for a suggested donation of ten dollars. The staff put drops of paint on five-inch by seven-inch canvases inside plastic bags, then placed catnip and treats on top of the bags and let the cats do their thing. Some cats sat on top of the plastic, others moved around, and others laid on top of the plastic. They produced various patterns of abstract art.

During my shift at the open house, I browsed the artwork. One image drew me in by Kiku, a black shorthair with dreamy green eyes. In her work, I saw a bird on a branch in a tree. I thought of a colorful parrot perched in a tree in the tropics and wondered if Kiku was thinking about birds when she was working on this piece.

I bought her painting.

After leaving Animal Aid that day, I stopped at a supermarket to stock up. During checkout, I felt compelled to show Kiku's artwork to the clerk. He looked at the painting while scanning my groceries and complimented Kiku's abilities.

Before the clerk's shift, he was at the animal hospital with his seven-year-old Newfoundland, who was very sick. There was nothing the vet could do, so the dog had to be euthanized. "I have been distracted today thinking about it," he said.

"I understand," I replied. "It's never easy saying good-bye to our furry companions."

"Thank you for showing me the painting," he said. "It cheered me up."

I never saw Kiku at the shelter again because she found her forever home. Her painting has a home, too, on the top shelf of a bookcase in my living room.

Kiku's masterpiece

Kisses

I parked along one of the spurs leading to the roundabout in a quaint neighborhood in Portland. Beautiful, well-kept homes dating from the 1940s lined the streets shaded in maples and firs. I walked to the roundabout, its heart filled with roses in full bloom. Ladd Circle Park and Rose Garden, the heart of the neighborhood.

The garden was a series of small beds with rose bushes that sometimes reached over my head. Yellow roses in one bed, lavender in another, yellow in another, red in another, and miniature roses with red and white patterns that reminded me of peppermints in a candy jar.

I stopped in a row of pink roses. The sun's rays kissed the raindrops, which sparkled like crystals. The roses were kissed twice that day from the gentle rain that quenched their thirst and the sun that gave them light to grow.

Rose covered in raindrops at Ladd Circle Park and Rose Garden in Portland, Oregon

Life Cycles

I'm driving on a backroad through open range at dusk in the southwestern high desert while my friend watches the scenery from the passenger side. We approach a herd of Angus cattle grazing along the right side of the road.

"Oh, look at the cows," she says while I'm focusing on the road, so I almost jump out of my seat. "I want to say 'hi' to them," meaning she wants me to stop so she can get out of the car.

"I'm staying in the car," I say. I grew up on a farm, where we raised Angus cattle, so I have no interest in greeting them. Likely the feeling is mutual. My friend is from the city.

I pull over. She gets out of the car and walks along the shoulder behind the car. Seconds later, she rushes back to the car, opens the door, points toward a bush, and says, "There's a sick cow lying over there. What do we do?"

"Is the cow lying on its stomach or on its side?" I ask.

"It's lying over there. It isn't moving."

I couldn't see it. "If it's lying on its stomach, it's okay. If it's lying on its side, it's dead."

She shuts the door and disappears in the same direction. I stay in the car. Five minutes later, she returns, sits in the passenger seat, and closes the door.

"Did you say 'hello' to them?"

"Yeah, but they ran away." She pauses, then says, "That cow is dead. I could see its ribs. What should we do?"

"There's nothing we can do."

"Shouldn't we tell someone?"

"Who would we tell? We don't know who the owners are. Besides, they'll probably leave it there so the coyotes and vultures can eat it."

She looks at me as if I just flew in from another galaxy.

The next day, we go on a horseback ride with a local guide. During our ride, she mentions the dead cow near the side of the road north of town.

"Oh, yeah, that's my father-in-law's herd," the guide says. "He knows about it. He'll leave it there for the coyotes to feed on. They need to eat, too."

Mockingbird

The mockingbird sings
Perched on a branch above us
In the old oak tree.

He stops and listens,
Memorizes what he heard,
Then echoes the sounds.

We listen in awe
As we wait for the school bus
To whisk us away.

At school, we're learning
While the mockingbird listens,
Records, and repeats.

My Favorite Road Sign

Nurselogs

1

When I first heard the term, "nurselog," a long time ago, I couldn't fathom it. A log could be a piece of wood someone throws in a stove, fireplace, or a firepit at a campsite to stay warm. A log could be a toy in the woods, where children and dogs, or even adults, romp and play on and around it. Many logs could be used to build a house or cabin. Or it might be a bench in a park or carved into a canoe or totem pole.

But a nurselog? It's about nourishment. It's about the cycle of life – a dying being giving itself to plants, insects, animals, and other organisms to thrive. It's about creating a small world in a bigger one to sustain others.

2

Mushrooms love dark, moist places—among them, nurselogs. They grow on top and on the side of these fallen tree trunks in the forest. They play peek-a-boo under the logs, where they root under the logs and lean out toward the light they need to grow. They don't need much light.

3
Every nurselog I've seen is covered in moss. Moss and mushrooms share their love for moist environments, but moss can grow in the light and dark—anywhere that's wet most of the time. Moss nurtures other plants and attracts insects, which helps the mini world of the nurselog expand more.

4
Seedlings love nurselogs. The decaying bark, moss, leaves, and needles that settle on the log give them food to grow and sprout into a plant or tree. The trees that begin their lives on nurselogs stretch their roots along and around the log and feed from the log as the log deteriorates, then anchor themselves in the earth.

A mature nurselog in the Hall of Mosses in the Hoh Rain Forest in Olympic National Park

A new nurselog on the Mini Trail in the Hoh Rain Forest in Washington's Olympic National Park

Perfectly Imperfect

It hangs on a wall built of logs in the chapel at Shadowcliff Lodge in Grand Lake, Colorado—a photo of a mountain printed on canvas and stretched over a wooden frame.

The mountain of beige rock with a jagged peak is almost naked. The few clothes it wears are stunted pines in its cracks.

More pines grow from the parched soil at the base of the mountain, but in the foreground stands one tall tree with bare branches, except for the lowest one, where a large pom-pom of dead needles clings to the edge.

Someone hung this photo crooked, so from where I sit, the base of the mountain is level with the chapel floor.

I remember my art class in high school, where I drew a pine tree in front of our building in pencil on an eight-and-a-half by 11-inch piece of typing paper. The pine tree was perfect—thick, full needles and shaped symmetrically—except for one branch void of needles on the bottom branch. This branch was in the same location as the branch of the bare pine tree with the dead needles in the photo in the chapel.

When Mr. Marler, my art teacher, returned my piece, I saw a tiny A- written in pencil in the bottom right corner. After class, he said, "I love your picture, but why didn't you finish it?"

"I did," I replied. "It's a drawing of the pine tree in the front yard of the high school—the one at the top of the stairs."

He nodded.

Both trees and the mountain are beautiful as they are, perfectly imperfect as nature intended.

A bent tree in Great Smoky Mountains National Park in Tennessee

Sea Lion Zen

Sea lions at Cape Arago State Park near Charleston, Oregon

Seeing through the Storm

The dark clouds are building over the mountains in the distance. I'm watching the streaks under their bellies move closer, wondering how much longer I can enjoy the view of the lake before they sneeze all over me. Those same clouds and the mountains reflect in the lake, but the closer the clouds come, the more the darkness chases the mirror away.

The darkness begins to reveal a different view of the lake—a crystal ball clearly showing steelhead swimming above the bed of pebbles and sand. They aren't in a hurry to go anywhere. Maybe it's because they know no one will try to catch them with a storm approaching. They can meander for a few hours and just be fish.

Their movements mesmerize me, and I begin to wonder why humans are always in such a rush. I would have missed this beautiful moment if I hadn't stopped at the pullout to make pictures of the view. The reflection of the mountains in the lake drew me in.

Maybe what I really needed to see is the crystal ball the clouds created. It's a key to slow down and savor the present.

Clouds rising from Mount Hood near Portland, Oregon

Shopping for Pants at a French Market

I'm on a mission this sunny Wednesday morning in Collioure, France. Today, the market is open across from my hotel room, so I must buy two more pairs of the pants I found there on Sunday. They're made of light, soft fabric with an elastic band and wide flared legs that invite the breezes blowing off the Mediterranean Sea inside to cool my skin. One pair is black and the other matches the color of cow's cream. And they're the most comfortable pants I've ever worn.

These pants are substitutes for my poor wardrobe decisions back home in Vancouver, Washington. When I packed for this trip, I grabbed my only two pairs of shorts in the closet. Wearing shorts west of the Cascade Mountains isn't a common occurrence because the weather is usually too cold.

I assumed the shorts would still fit, but when I slipped on a pair after my overnight flight from Portland to Barcelona, they wouldn't stay up. That's because I've lost twenty pounds during the past year—a directive from my doctor to improve my health. I mentally kicked myself for not trying them on before I left. What the heck was I thinking? Apparently I wasn't.

For four days, I toured Barcelona, Bagá, d'Ax Les Thermes, and Andorra, while my shorts drooped below my waist and I constantly pulled them up. I feared they'd fall off, and they almost did a few times. How embarrassing that would be, standing in my T-shirt and underwear in a foreign country with my shorts bunched around my ankles. What would people think?

Clothing for sale at an open-air market in Collioure, France

One of the tour guides in Spain wore the same style of pants I bought on Sunday. When I first saw them, I fell in love and became determined to find some of my own as soon as possible. They looked comfortable and would be perfect for the hot weather. I could also wear them on future trips.

Now I'm crossing the cobblestone bridge to the open-air market in a plaza shared with the Petit Train. I walk past food trucks selling paella, cheese, and chicken, but the aromas don't tantalize my senses because my sniffer is broken, thanks to a nasty bout with the flu in 2014. Usually I imagine what the foods smell like, but I can't linger today. I have only twenty minutes to complete my mission. The writing workshop awaits back at the hotel—although Karen, our workshop leader, won't mind if I'm fashionably late. I'd fit in with the French's sense of time, but my Midwestern upbringing conflicts with this cultural value.

"Always be on time. Early is better," Grandma and Mom drilled into my brain since as long as I can remember.

Now I'm in the row of vendor tents with white canopies supported by four steel poles, one in each corner. Bright yellow, green, red, and blue bowls catch my eye in one tent, luring me to browse, but I resist. I must find the man who sold the pants to me on Sunday. The last time I saw him, his tent was the next to the last one on the left side of the row.

East of the bowl tent, the tents flanking the row until the end of the cobblestone trail are filled with clothes—all for women, all light, breezy blouses, shorts, and dresses perfect for the Collioure climate. Again, I'm tempted to stop, but I must move on. I can browse if there's time left after I complete my mission.

Another ten feet away, I see the merchant's tent in the same place on the left, but it looks much different. On Sunday, it was packed with so many racks filled with clothing, I barely could squeeze through. Now, my scanning estimates that there are half as many today.

I look for a rack with the pants. It's gone. How can that be? Did the man sell all those pants on Sunday? I was the only person looking at them then. The rack was half full of solid pastel colors; the rest were either navy blue, black, or flower patterns.

Now, what do I do? This is why I came here again. My mission failed. My body tenses while I look around the tent with desperation and despair flooding my mind like a king tide on the Oregon Coast.

Then I turn and see a round rack directly ahead with straight-legged pants in different lengths and solid colors of sky blue, white, denim, and sea green. Surely some of my pants are in there. I must take a closer look, but time is quickly running out. Ten minutes left on the clock…

I dash to the rack. One hand frantically pushes each hanger to the left while the other hand pulls up a leg to examine it like a machine on a manufacturing line. None match my pants until I'm almost completely around the circle, where one pair of bright red pants and another pair of orange pants are waiting for me. They're the only ones on the rack matching the style of the pants I already have.

But there's a problem: I never wear brightly colored pants. I don't want to draw attention to my body—especially my big hips. Throughout junior high and during my freshman year in high school, I was obese, and the other kids laughed at me. I tried to ignore them, but it was hard to do when they wouldn't stop their taunts. My confidence waned, and since then, I've considered myself unattractive.

Do I buy them anyway? I think about conversations with Karen, her husband Jarrod, and the writing group about how the French aren't self-conscious about their bodies. They wear whatever they want and don't care what others think about it. Maybe I should be more like the French. Maybe this is a sign that I need to stop caring about what others think about my body.

When I return to the hotel, I roll up the pants and tuck them away in my suitcase. I'll wear them in Paris, my next stop after Collioure. What better place to make a statement and be ignored? I'm looking forward to it.

Slow Ride

This piece contains 15 song titles related to driving. How many can you spot? The answer key is on page 66.

Here I am, on the road again, navigating the famous Seattle-area traffic jams on the way home after working for a client on the Eastside. The DJs on KZOK, the classic rock station, have a warped sense of humor during rush hour. Today, the guy on air plays, "Slow Ride," when I'm stopped in traffic on the I-90 floating bridge. Slow cars, slow taxis, slow trucks—we're all living on a prayer.

There's no way I can drive 55 today in my car that looks nothing like a little red Corvette, and I can't get no satisfaction in this slog, except for looking forward to eventually making it home to West Seattle. At this rate, I'll probably drive all night. I can't take it easy.

How many more songs will this DJ play with a driving theme? Who knows! My head is full of them because I have nothing better to do where the streets have no name. I'm definitely not getting around this way. Apparently life is a highway in this DJ's world.

I hope my car isn't running on empty before I run down a dream or make it home, whichever comes first. There must be a bright side of the road.

Oh, look, there's an opening! It's time to shut up and drive.

Driver in Havana, Cuba

Song titles used in this piece:

1. On the Road Again—Willie Nelson
2. Slow Ride—Foghat
3. Living on a Prayer—Bon Jovi
4. I Can't Drive 55—Sammy Hagar
5. Little Red Corvette—Prince
6. (I Can't Get No) Satisfaction—Rolling Stones
7. I Drove All Night—Cyndi Lauper
8. Take It Easy—The Eagles
9. Where the Streets Have No Name—U2
10. I Get Around—The Beach Boys
11. Life is a Highway—Tom Cochrane
12. Runnin' Down a Dream—Tom Petty
13. Running on Empty—Jackson Browne
14. Bright Side of the Road—Van Morrison
15. Shut Up and Drive—Rihanna

Spring Haiku

No leaves in late April
But now they fully clothe the branches
In Minneapolis

More green in the park
Contrasting cherry sculpture
Strangely beautiful

Alone in quiet
Except for the birds singing
In the high branches

Peacefulness consoles
On this sunny city day
With urban nature

"Spoonbridge and Cherry" sculpture by Claes Oldenburg in the Sculpture Garden at Loring Park in Minneapolis

The Bird Emergency

Joe and I meet on campus one Saturday morning for a long walk and to hang out for the day. He isn't my boyfriend; we're just buddies who enjoy hanging out together.

Joe is an avid birder and talented artist. He draws his subjects with black ink on the tablets from the art supply section in the college bookstore. His details are meticulous. Every time I see one of his drawings, I expect the bird to fly off the page.

After a couple of hours walking the sidewalks crossing the campus lawns and wandering through the neighborhoods of houses dating from the 1920s and streets lined with oaks, maples, and elms, we decide to take a bathroom break at my apartment.

Minutes after we arrive, my phone rings. I pick up.

"Hey, Cheryl, it's Greg, Joe's friend. Is he there?"

I'm surprised Greg asked for Joe or even knew Joe was here. (This is long before cell phones were popular.) Joe must have told Greg what he was doing before he left home this morning.

"He is," I reply. "Would you like to talk to him?"

"Yes. It's important."

I hand the receiver to Joe. He stands at my tiny phone table, listening to Greg and occasionally saying, "uh-huh." Then he starts pacing as far as he can without pulling the phone cradle off the table. His responses to whatever Greg is saying change to:

"What?"

"Seriously?"

Hummingbird at Shore Acres State Park near Charleston, Oregon

"Oh, wow! We'll be right there!"

Joe hangs up and grabs his jacket. "We need to leave now. There's an emergency at Greg's house!"

"What happened?" I ask. "Are Greg and his wife okay?"

"They're okay," Joe says as he rushes to the door.

"Then, what's the emergency?"

"There's a rare bird in their backyard!"

We run the block and a half to Greg and Amy's house. Greg answers and lets us in, saying in a whisper as we tiptoe through the living room, "It's at our feeder outside the kitchen window—a male ruby-throated hummingbird."

Joe's eyes light up as he repeats, "A male ruby-throated hummingbird. I've never seen one!"

In the kitchen, Amy stands in front of the sink, quietly watching the feeder. We stop next to her and nod a greeting, then all four of us focus on the hummingbird drinking sugar water from the feeder hanging from the eave on the other side of the kitchen window. The window is about two feet across, so we stand in a horizontal line, touching each other with our arms and shoulders, watching this tiny creature flit to the feeder with wings flapping so fast they seem transparent, sip with wings in motion, back away from the feeder about a foot, then repeat. His head and beak are black and the red feathers around his neck remind me of a bandana. The rest of his feathers are gray, and those on his back turn an iridescent green when the light shines on them.

Time stops while we stand there, transfixed on the bird like a cat whose radar is locked in on its prey, except we're not pouncing on him. We're in his world, witnessing every second, quietly rooting for him with every nourishing drink, wondering whether he ever rests, appreciating him for who he is, and wishing him well in the giant world surrounding him.

Then he suddenly flies away. We're still frozen there, holding our breaths, anticipating his return. He didn't. Did he know we were watching him? If he could see us, what did he think about our fascination with him? We'll never know.

We break from our trances, and I look at the clock. Forty-five minutes have passed. We say our good-byes and resume our lives.

After I transfer to another college, I lose contact with Joe. Years later while browsing a gift shop in Joseph, Oregon, I see a book about birds in northeastern Oregon. I pick up the book and open it. The birds are illustrated with drawings, and the drawing style of the birds seems familiar, so I stop flipping the pages and look closer for a signature, and there it is—Joe's name penned in tiny cursive. I smile, delighted that my long-lost friend can share his talents as an artist and passion for birds with the world. I've found him again.

The Boy at the Market

When the open-air market opens this hot sunny morning in the cobblestone plaza across from my hotel room in Collioure, France, I stop at a merchant's tent to buy some shorts. I pull a pair of navy-blue shorts with a white anchor pattern from the rack, then look for one more pair in a different color.

Suddenly someone starts chattering behind me. I turn and see a boy who's probably twelve, with short blond hair and a tan matching a baguette crust. He's talking to me in rapid-fire French, gesturing toward the shorts I'm holding.

What does he want? My French is beyond fractured. From his tones, I sense he's repeating something.

I respond with hand signals. "I want to buy these," I say by holding the shorts against my heart, followed by drawing a circle with my free hand to relay, "but I'm still looking."

He doesn't understand. He continues the chatter, then reaches out like he's trying to snatch the shorts from me.

If he wants to buy a pair, why doesn't he grab one from the rack? There are at least a dozen hanging there in the same pattern and style.

I panic from his persistence. Horrible thoughts swirl in my head. Is browsing illegal? I thought the French want shoppers to linger. Nothing rushes in this village, except the words flying from this kid's mouth.

Will he call the patrol who's in training maneuvers this week and tell them to take me away? I'll be the topic of tomorrow's front-page article in the local newspaper: "American woman arrested for violating French shopping etiquette."

This can't happen. In desperation, I launch Google Translate on my phone and type, "I want to buy these shorts, but I'm still looking." I step next to him and point to the French translation. He glances at it, then continues repeating the words I'll never understand.

My panic becomes anger. Why doesn't this pesky kid leave? Is taunting a tourist his preferred entertainment? Surely there are other things he can do.

A tall, tan woman with blonde hair enters the tent. The boy stops talking. She looks at the translation on my phone and notices the shorts in my hand.

"Are you sure you picked the right size?" she asks. She holds up the tag, which reads "M/L," medium to large.

"Non," I say, then return the shorts to the rack and find a matching pair in the appropriate size.

"I want to buy these, but I'm still shopping," I say. She nods and leaves, but the boy stares at me. He's quiet now, thank God.

I grab another pair of shorts in a flower print and search for a place to pay. The woman is organizing a rack of clothes nearby, so I ask her.

"You may pay me," she says.

When the transaction is done, I return to the hotel, relieved that I'm still a free woman who will soon be a cool woman—after I change.

La Plage Rouge, a shop in Collioure, France

Face Rock on the Oregon Coast

The Face in the Rock

My bare feet tingle from the cold, shallow layer of water over soft sand as I navigate the obstacle course of black rocks along the shore at Face Rock State Park in Bandon, Oregon. In the distance, I see another rock, a face silhouette, staring at the northern sky. The mouth gapes, and the endless ocean's roar drowns its voice until the gulls speak in its place.

Early the next morning during low tide, the Sandman comes with his crew, drawing a labyrinth of circles in the sand, outlining them with more circles and connecting them with curved lines. I watch from the bluff until they finish, then descend the trail to walk through the labyrinth and meditate on the sounds of the waves, the gulls, and the foghorns in the distance where the rock stares upward, mouth frozen open.

A few feet behind me, a man with a chest-long brown beard and shoulder-length hair, dressed in a Northwest flannel shirt and faded blue jeans, marches through the labyrinth, playing a pan flute while others follow him.

I leave the labyrinth and return to the top of the bluff when the tide begins to rise. Soon, the waves erase the labyrinth, the circles in the sand. The slate is ready for a new drawing when the Sandman returns.

The face in the rock remains behind, still, staring silently, endlessly into the northern sky.

Circles in the Sand at Face Rock State Park in Bandon, Oregon

For more information about the labyrinths at Face Rock State Park, visit Circles in the Sand at sandypathbandon.com.

The Building Inspector

This story answers the question: What could happen if the wolf in the children's story, "The Three Little Pigs," changed his behavior?

"I'm probably risking my political career by doing this," Mayor Hogwash said, "but you came highly recommended."

Warford Wolf scratched his hairy chin with his claws. "I assure you, Mr. Mayor, I am not a threat to anyone. My meat-eating days are over."

Mayor Hogwash turned his chair toward the window, wiggled his snout, and rubbed his chin with a hoof. While the mayor stared at the maple trees blazing in red, orange, and yellow, Warford wondered what he was thinking. Warford really needed this job. Work had been hard to find since he finished the apprenticeship with Buford Boar at Pigsty Gulch. He was grateful Buford trusted him and took the risk to train him. In return, Warford worked hard and showed Buford he could be an outstanding building inspector. Although all the pigs respected Buford there and treated him like family, thanks to Buford's faith in him, no one outside the village believed a wolf would never eat them, so the job rejections continued to pile up.

The minute Mayor Hogwash contemplated the scenery in the courthouse yard felt like an eternity. Warford's body stiffened when the mayor swiveled his chubby body dressed in a suit and tie to face the wolf again.

"Well, I can't prolong this any longer," Mayor Hogwash said. "We desperately need a building inspector, and you're our only qualified candidate. How soon can you start?"

"How about tomorrow morning?" Warford started to smile but checked himself. He didn't want his big, sharp teeth to show. His beautiful smile received many compliments from the pack—when he was in one—but he was kicked out when he became a vegetarian. He lost the desire to hunt and kill prey after a horrible incident ten years ago with the pigs in a town very similar to Hogtown. Those events still haunted him in his dreams. That's when he promised himself to never hurt a pig again and to help keep them safe by becoming a building inspector.

"Great! Pauline Piglet, my assistant, will give you details on the first buildings you'll inspect in the morning. Be here at nine o'clock sharp."

"Thank you, Mr. Mayor. You won't be disappointed. Before I leave today, I'd like to review the building codes to give me a head start."

"No problem. Pauline will show you where they are."

The mayor walked Warford to the door of his office and bumped elbows with him before Warford departed. Trying to simulate human handshaking with hooves and paws with sharp claws was too painful.

Warford's first building on the list was Hog Heaven, a new market consisting of a tin shed with a canvas awning. Shelves and coolers were lined neatly along the wall of the shed under the awning, filled with cans and boxes of food.

When Warford arrived, he saw Sam Shank, the owner, sorting fruits and vegetables under the awning and arranging them in neat rows and piles in the bins. Warford had never seen such colorful, fresh produce and wondered where Sam found it. Warford struggled to keep his mouth from watering while he made a mental note to return after work today and stock up.

Warford walked over to Sam to introduce himself. When Sam saw him, he rushed behind the counter, pulled a baseball bat from a shelf under the cash register, and gripped it between the toes on his front hooves.

"What do you want?" Sam demanded, glaring at Warford. "If you move any closer, I'll smash your head in."

Warford stopped and held up a paw. "Hey, I'm not here to harm you. I'm the new building inspector. Mayor Hogwash sent me here to inspect your building."

"That's hard to believe. Mayor Hogwash has some strange ideas, but hiring a wolf? That's over the top—not in good way. I can't understand why he was elected."

Warford didn't want to talk politics with Sam. He was here to do his job. Besides, he saw from the town's records that Sam moved here three months ago, so Sam wasn't in Hogtown during the last mayoral and city council elections.

"I'll show you my ID if you'll allow me to come closer," Warford said.

Sam raised the bat over his head, ready to swing. His apron strings in the back loosened, and it dangled over his short-sleeved, button-down shirt like a giant bib.

"How can I trust you? I heard about that incident in Porkville."

That comment hit Warford harder than any bat ever would. Why would any of the pigs here trust him? They didn't know him like the residents of Pigsty Gulch.

Warford pulled his badge from his denim overall bib with his right front paw and stretched out his leg as far as he could reach. "Here's my ID. Can you see it? It has my name, title, photo, badge number, and the City of Hogtown logo. If you still don't believe me, call city hall."

Sam stared at Warford's ID, then lowered the bat but continued to grip it tightly in front of him. "Okay, get on with it. Just stay away from me and my customers. I don't want us to be your lunch."

"Don't worry. I'm a vegetarian."

"Then stay away from my produce!"

Warford checked the inside and outside of the market. Everything seemed to be structurally sound, but there was one final test he used to make extra sure. He huffed, puffed, and blew on the building, and within seconds, strips of metal flew everywhere. The bins where the beautiful produce was neatly organized toppled over, spilling their contents. Sam dropped his bat and ran behind a rock.

When the commotion settled, Sam screamed from his hiding place, "What do you think you're doing? You destroyed my store!"

"I was testing the building to determine how well it would withstand a heavy windstorm," Warford replied. "You should know they're common in the winter around here."

"I'm not from here! I moved here three months ago. You have no right to blow down my store!"

"Your market wouldn't have survived the first windstorm this winter. Those storms are stronger than my breath ever will be. My job is to keep you safe."

"Well, this is a lousy way to do it! I'm reporting this to the mayor!" Sam threw his apron in the grass, stomped to Hogtown City Hall, and disappeared inside.

The next two inspections didn't go any better for the building owners. Warford's second stop was at a new unoccupied housing development, Wheyward Downs. Several pigs put down payments on the houses and were waiting for the construction to end so they could move in. The homes built of straw and mud couldn't withstand Warford's strong lungs for more than a minute.

The third stop was at the mayor's new mansion, which was built of stucco. When Warford blew on it, it survived longer than the new houses, but only a minute longer.

By then, the word spread across town and throughout the region, and everyone was angry. Sam and Harry Hampshire, the housing development contractor, threatened to sue the town. Mayor Hogwash was furious with Warford for destroying his new mansion. He asked Pauline to find Warford and tell him to return to his office now.

"Do you have any idea what you've done?" Mayor Hogwash yelled at Warford from his desk before Warford could cross the threshold to the mayor's office. "The entire town is mad at me, and now I have citizens threatening to sue. And you blew down my new home! What were you thinking?"

Warford stood in front of the desk, watching the mayor while trying to maintain his composure. In his old life, he would have eaten Sam and the mayor without a second thought. Pigs directing anger at him in his old world caused him to react swiftly without thinking. The stress today tempted him to revert, but he must remain strong. He hadn't come this far to destroy his new life.

Before speaking, Warford practiced a mind-calming technique his therapist, Sally Sow, taught him in Pigsty Gulch when he was under stress. He visualized sitting on the shore of a lake with the full moon reflecting on the ripples dancing in the water. Then he took a deep breath, looked at the moon, and exhaled while howling in his mind, which released his stress and his old desires.

"With all due respect, Mr. Mayor, I was only doing my job," Warford said. "Today, I carried out my inspections based on my experience and best practices in the industry. When the windstorms come this winter, none of those buildings I blew down would have survived."

"I have never heard of any inspectors trying to blow down buildings to test their structural integrity," the mayor said, "which makes me question yours."

"I understand your concerns, Mr. Mayor, but the buildings aren't strong enough because of the building codes. According to the codes, the residents can use any type of material to build, and the requirements for structural integrity aren't clear."

Mayor Hogwash slammed one hoof down on his desk as his face reddened deeper than an apple skin. The sudden noise caused Warford to jump.

"How dare you criticize my building codes! I wrote those codes!"

A full moon near Billings, Montana

Warford took a deep breath before replying with, "Sir, I'm not critiquing your writing. I'm just saying—"

Mayor Hogwash's eyes widened so much that Warford expected them to pop out of his head and roll off the desk.

"I don't care what you're saying!" The mayor pointed a hoof at the door. "Get out of my office *now*! And don't ever come back!"

Devastated, Warford returned to Pigsty Gulch. He was too ashamed to face his friends. Instead, he spent most of his time sleeping in his den. When he was awake, he read, and when he needed groceries, he shopped in another town where no one would recognize him. It was too cold to start a garden or build a greenhouse. Maybe he could build one in the spring so he could become more self-sufficient. Maybe he could experiment with different vegetable and herb combinations, publish a vegetarian cookbook, and become a famous chef. Maybe another career change would be good for him, but he regretted giving up as a building inspector after all the training and support he'd received.

Meanwhile in Hogtown, the winter storms arrived. The winds were stronger than usual this year, so by the time they passed through, most of the homes and businesses were damaged or destroyed. Mayor Hogwash and the city council struggled to find enough supplies to help the citizens rebuild. The delays angered everyone. Bert Berkshire, a highly respected mechanic in Hogtown, formed a political action group, and volunteers began gathering signatures on a petition to oust the mayor and all the city council members in a recall election.

The city council called a meeting, where they threatened to remove Mayor Hogwash. "This could have been prevented," Holly Yorkshire, the most outspoken member, said to the mayor. "We need stronger building codes. How many times have we talked about this?"

The mayor sighed. Holly was right. This was discussed at several city council meetings, but he refused to listen to Holly and the other concerned council members. Eventually the topic was dropped from the agenda. Warford pointed out problems with the codes, too, and the mayor responded by firing him.

After the meeting, the mayor stopped at Pauline's desk. "I want you to find that wolf," he said. "Tell him to come to my office immediately."

When Warford arrived in Hogtown, he was saddened to see cracked and crumbling houses and businesses and rubble scattered everywhere. He noticed one of the warehouses that survived the storms had been turned into a homeless shelter. Some families who lost their homes pitched tents on their property or slept in their cars. The city hall building didn't suffer any damage, except for a few broken windows on the top floor that were boarded up.

As soon as Warford walked into the reception area, Mayor Hogwash opened his office door and motioned for Warford to come in and sit in front of his desk. Then the mayor sat behind his desk and gazed at Warford for at least a minute. The silence felt much longer to Warford, and he almost spoke up just to calm his nerves.

"I made a terrible mistake, and the citizens of this town are suffering for it," the mayor finally said. "You were right, but I was too angry to listen to you. I should never have sent you on those building inspections until the codes were updated."

Warford's muscles relaxed as the mayor continued.

"I would like to hire you back as the building inspector. But I don't want you to inspect any more buildings until you and I can review the codes and improve them. If it helps, I will raise your salary by twenty percent. What do you say…will you help us?"

Warford couldn't suppress his smile this time. "I would be honored, Mr. Mayor." He can follow his dream after all!

The mayor smiled and then bumped elbows with Warford. "Great! Let's get started tomorrow. I'll see you here in the morning, nine o'clock sharp."

During the next three months, Warford and the mayor reviewed and revised the building codes, and the city council approved them unanimously. The residents of Pigsty Gulch donated supplies to help Hogtown rebuild and encouraged other towns in the region to contribute. The pigs' respect for Warford grew in Hogtown, and at the next community service banquet, they gave him the Citizen of the Year award.

The Feline Arbitrator

The stress was always high during my remote contract for a large software company, but the approaching holiday season accelerated the pressure. Upper management expected our four-person editing team to finish 6,000 pages of content in four weeks—an all-time record. And, to make matters worse, all the edited content must be released by New Year's Eve.

If that wasn't enough, a project manager who worked with my supervisor wanted to "borrow" our team for an urgent special assignment—also requested by upper management. This project manager wasn't very organized, and so this supposedly small project turned into a full-time affair. So far, we had lost a week of editing time, and no end was in sight. By the middle of the second week, the editors became so frustrated, we threatened mutiny.

In an attempt to save the sinking ship, my supervisor scheduled a two-hour teleconference. I moved my laptop from my desk to the kitchen counter, where my speaker phone was connected, to work while listening to the conversation.

TC, my shorthaired brown tabby, relaxed in his usual spot in the living room, on top of his scratching post. He was strategically positioned to watch the birds and squirrels through the sliding door to the patio, yet keep an eye on me at the kitchen counter and nap in between. When the call started, he was asleep.

An hour into the two-hour conversation, when tensions were at their highest, TC awoke to the ruckus. When he detected the noise was coming from a black object on the counter and my attention was glued to it, he jumped on the kitchen counter and sniffed the phone's handset, keypad, and speaker.

Then he pointed his nose directly at the speaker and said, "Meow."

Everyone stopped talking. I held my breath, fearing what would happen next.

TC looked at me with his big green eyes, as if he were saying, "There!" Then he jumped off the counter and climbed to the top of his scratching post to resume his nap.

The ten-second pause felt like an eternity. My supervisor broke the silence with, "Is…that…a…CAT?"

"Yes," I replied. "It's my cat. He jumped on the counter."

Everyone laughed while my supervisor yelled, "Sign an NDA (non-disclosure agreement) for that cat!"

When we regained our composure, the conversation continued cordially and professionally, and we reached an agreement. We would quickly proofread the pages and flag any developmental edits for the next revision. If we could finish all the work by December 22, then we could take our holiday breaks. To help us make the shortened deadline, my supervisor hired more editors.

We finished a day early.

Our team continued working together afterward without TC's intervention. But we often recalled TC's comment on that cold December day and laughed about his impromptu role as a feline arbitrator.

TC, The Feline Arbitrator

The Ghost of Golden

The weathered, abandoned buildings in a field east of Wolf Creek, Oregon, intrigued me. I pulled my car next to a dark brown sign and parked. "Golden, Oregon," was centered across the top of the sign in white capital letters.

I read the text under the title and learned that Golden is a ghost town. It started as a mining camp in the 1850s during the gold rush and became an official town of 100 people around 1890. Unlike almost all gold rush towns, it was not rowdy because saloons were not allowed. Two churches served the town.

I got out of the car and walked around the four weathered buildings in a field of ankle-high grass surrounded by Douglas firs. Although the town looked abandoned, it appeared someone was keeping the buildings maintained. I peeked inside the largest building, which might have been a mercantile. Through the smudged glass windows, I saw supplies scattered in one room. The other rooms I could see were empty.

I walked to the church, with gray boards and a steeple that was in excellent shape. I climbed the steps to the entrance and saw a sign at the right of the door with the service schedule. Services are held here every Sunday.

Who would drive all this way to go to a church service when no one lives here?

I peeked inside. The pine-stained walls, wooden benches, and pulpit had been restored. The windows looked brand new.

The church in Golden, Oregon

Curious, I reached for the doorknob and tried to turn it. The knob moved and released the latch in the doorframe. I pulled the door partway open, walked inside, and wandered around the chapel. When I finished, I stopped in a back corner to take some pictures.

I heard the sound of a truck engine, which stopped in front of the church, followed by the clomp, clomp of boots climbing the stairs. Just before the boots reached the porch, my camera's flash went off. The light briefly flooded the chapel.

"Whoa," a shaky male voice said, and the boots retreated down the stairs.

I rushed to the porch, holding my camera. By then, the tall man wearing blue jeans, a checkered flannel shirt, and tan cowboy boots had his old black Chevy truck door open and was about to climb into the cab.

"I'm sorry I scared you," I called out from the top of the stairs.

He turned around, his tanned, weathered face full of fright. When he noticed I was a real human, relief washed away the fear. He smiled and rubbed his short brown beard.

"I wasn't expecting that," he said.

He glanced across the road and saw the Washington state plate on the back of my Honda CR-V. "Are you visiting?" he asked.

"Yes, my mother lives in Glendale," I said. "She's working today in Wolf Creek, so I'm exploring the area until she comes home."

"Where does she work?" the man asked. "I live in Wolf Creek."

"She's a seamstress at Select Designs."

"I know the owners," he said. "They've been there for a long time."

"My mother has worked there for five years."

The man looked up at the steeple.

"Is someone restoring this town?" I asked. "The buildings are in good shape, especially this church."

"Yeah, a committee is working with the state parks department to restore it. The parks department owns the town now. I'm on the restoration committee and came out to check on the steeple. We hired someone to work on it last week."

"That's quite a project. It will be nice when it's done."

"It will. We still have a lot of work to do, as you can see."

"It's always worth the effort, preserving history."

The man nodded. "Well, I'd better get back to town. Nice to meet you."

"Nice to meet you, too. I'll be more careful with my flash the next time."

He chuckled, climbed into the truck, and drove toward Wolf Creek.

That's when I remembered that I didn't ask for his name. I thought about other times I've had conversations with strangers and we become so engrossed in our exchange that we forget to introduce ourselves. I've remembered so many of these conversations long after we parted and wonder if our paths will ever cross again. So far, they haven't.

Historical marker at the Golden townsite

The Girl on the Ferry

On my way home from work in Manhattan when I lived on Staten Island, a woman and her two daughters sat across from me. The mother, who was dressed as if she was returning home from an office, read the *New York Post* while her youngest daughter leaned on her arm. The oldest, who was probably ten years old, seemed bored. She sat next to me and started talking to me while sliding back and forth on the orange plastic bench.

"Where are you going?" she asked.

"I'm on my way home from work."

"Where do live?"

"I'm in Saint George, a short walk from the ferry terminal."

"Are you married?"

"Yes. My husband is a student at NYU."

She twisted on the seat as if she was trying to curl into a ball. Her black braids, with pink beads woven into them, bounced while she squirmed.

After she stopped and sat up straight next to me, she looked at me and said, "I have a cat."

"You do?"

"Yes. He's black-and white. His name is Tux."

"Tux. That's an interesting name."

"He looks like he's wearing a coat." She smiled.

"How old is he?"

"He's two."

"I have two cats."

She smiled again and her big brown eyes sparkled. "How old are they?"

"One is six, and the other one is eleven. Their names are TC and Tiger."

"Wow!"

She pondered my response for a minute, then yelled at her sister, "Hey! She has a cat that's older than you are!"

Her sister looked at her for a few seconds, then closed her eyes.

The Positive Side of Addiction

Dear REI,

Addiction isn't always negative. Hiking is my addiction, prompted by my first camping trip in Oregon's Eagle Cap Wilderness. During our steep, seven-mile trek to Echo Lake, we enjoyed spectacular views of a forested valley surrounded by mountains and a waterfall bordering the trail halfway through our hike. The trail ended at a flat, grassy field where the deep blue circle of Echo Lake contrasted with the greenery. Wildflowers dotted the field. Two gray, snowcapped Eagle Cap mountains provided an incredible backdrop. My memories of this first hike have driven me to follow other trails to experience the beauty and wonder of each. I can truly say this is my addiction, from which I'll never recover.

Cheryl Landes

This letter was originally published in the REI spring 1990 camping catalog.

Sunrise at the Continental Divide in Rocky Mountain National Park

Trillium at Great Smoky Mountains National Park in Tennessee

Trailheads

Trailheads are intriguing and alluring, not only because they start a journey, but also because there's the mystery of where they go. Sure, the signs with the trail names can give us clues, as well as any research we might have done before arriving there, but we don't really know what lies ahead of us. What we each experience is unique.

Maybe we want to follow a trail through the woods to see where it leads because there aren't any clues on that sign at the trailhead. Maybe someone recommended it. Maybe it's raining and we want to enjoy the water enhancing the green canopy and undergrowth while we hear the drops tap on the umbrella above our heads. Maybe we want to indulge our fascination with raindrops on the leaves and flower pedals. Maybe we want to look for birds watching us from the branches. Maybe we'll enter a clearing and see a bald eagle perched on a scraggy branch waiting to catch a salmon in the stream running alongside the trail.

Or maybe we're following a trail to the top of a mountain to soak in the view on a clear, sunny day. In this case, the trailhead sign probably gives us a clue about what's ahead. Maybe the sign will even show us how long it will take us to get there—either in minutes or miles, but most likely only miles. We start the walk, anticipating what we'll find until we arrive. Our reward is worth the quest.

Another type of trailhead is the entrance to the auto tour road at the Ridgefield National Wildlife Refuge in Ridgefield,

Washington—a four-mile loop where I use my car as a blind to watch birds who've stopped during the spring migration to rest and replenish on the abundant food. I drive slowly, looking for transient sandhill cranes, snow geese, and trumpeter swans, along with the herons, blackbirds, robins, and other creatures who call the refuge home year-round.

What are your favorite trailheads?

A foggy spring morning at the Ridgefield National Wildlife Refuge

A blue heron at the Ridgefield National Wildlife Refuge in Ridgefield, Washington

A trumpeter swan during the spring migration
at the Ridgefield National Wildlife Refuge

Who's that Hottie?

My 83-year-old mother and I just finished going through the drive-through at Arby's in Wenatchee, Washington, and were headed to a park along the Columbia River to enjoy lunch and the view. I stopped in the right lane at a five-way intersection and looked for traffic to clear before turning. Less than a quarter mile later, flashing lights from a police cruiser reflected in my rear-view mirror. All three lanes were full of cars, so I pulled into the parking lot of a gas station to allow the officer to pass.

The cruiser pulled up behind me and stopped. The policeman got out and walked toward my car.

"What did you do?" Mom asked.

"I don't know," I replied.

The officer was probably in his early to mid-30s. The black uniform accented his tanned skin, broad shoulders, trim abs, and well-defined arm muscles. His sunglasses matched the color of his uniform.

"Hi, how are you today?" he asked when he stopped outside my window. "I'm not giving you a ticket, but I wanted you to know that you turned right at an intersection where you can't turn on red."

I didn't see the sign and told him so (nicely, of course).

"But I still have to ask for your driver's license."

I handed my license to him. He walked to his cruiser to finish a background check, then returned and handed the license back to me.

"Are you visiting the area?" he asked.

"Yes, we arrived two days ago. We're spending another night here, then heading up to Omak for three days."

"Enjoy," he said. "Have a nice day."

After he left, Mom said, "He was a nice guy."

I agreed.

Then she said, "He's cute, too!"

Kayakers on the Columbia River at
Wenatchee Confluence State Park, Wenatchee, Washington

Sunset at Shore Acres State park near Charleston, Oregon

Sunsets

Sunsets carry memories. I think of the times my husband and I walked the beaches of the Oregon Coast at the end of the day during trips to visit his family. We'd sit on giant driftwood logs and talk about our dreams while the sun slid into the ocean. Often we stayed to watch the colors grow richer with the afterglow and surrender to the stars twinkling through a velvety canopy.

When we were at home in Seattle, we'd walk to the viewpoints in our neighborhood to watch the colors reflect in the skyscrapers across Elliot Bay and in the water in Puget Sound. When the sun descended, the Olympic Mountains transformed into a black silhouette in the distance. Many times, the beauty kept us speechless.

My husband left this planet in 2016, but I still think of him when I walk on familiar beaches and in our old neighborhood during my trips to Seattle. Those happy memories keep him alive in my heart. Sometimes it feels like he's walking alongside me.

Sunsets bring joy. One winter, I spent two months in Minneapolis. My client rented an apartment for me on the twenty-eighth floor of a high-rise, which faced the sunset side of downtown. Every night, the sky delivered a variety of patterns, ranging from layers on a cake to tiny stripes, swirls, wisps, and bright colors peeking above low clouds laced with a thin bright light. Every night, I watched the show from the windows in the living room as soon as I arrived from the office. Dinner always waited.

Sunsets bring comfort. Eight years after working in Minneapolis, I followed the Auto Road to the top of Mount Washington in New Hampshire during one of the clearest days I've seen there. It was late in the afternoon, so I couldn't spend much time on the mountain before the rangers told us to leave. On the way down, I stopped at a pullout after spotting a panorama reminding me of an impressionist painting: subtle layers of black and dark and light gray peaks bathed in a peachy lemon yellow hue as far as I could see.

Earlier that day, I left Maine, where a friend was losing her long battle with cancer. While I watched the mountain view from the open window of my rental car, a comforting presence washed over me and the wind said, "She's at peace." The next day, another friend in the same town sent an email with the time of her death. She departed the same moment the wind whispered to me and I wondered if she was the one who spoke to me, reassuring me she's free of suffering.

Sunsets bring excitement. One afternoon during a trip to Kauai, I went on a cruise along the southern side of the island. When we returned to Eleele, the sun painted the sky in the brightest colors I've seen. Feathery shapes of pink, orange, and yellow waved against a purplish-charcoal background. A layer of clouds lay low over the horizon, and the water glowed in orange and pink.

Sunset from the top of Mount Washington, New Hampshire

People watched from the dock and in the adjacent park. Some commented on the colors, while others just stood in silence and smiled. In the restaurant where I ate dinner, the servers and host stopped rushing for a minute to snap pictures with their phones. The energy from this experience renewed me after a week packed with workshops, a conference, and tourist activities squeezed in between.

Tonight in late October, I'm standing outside the Héraðsskólinn Historic Guesthouse in Laugarvatn, Iceland, watching the sun descend at the top of the hill. This is the first time I've seen a sunset here because of the cloud cover late every day. Now I watch purple swirls rise above a layer of charcoal, burnt orange, and gold, where a row of trees are silhouetted in the foreground. It's a beautiful ending to five days of relaxing, soaking in the geothermal springs, and writing. I'll carry the finished stories and ideas conceived until I find a home for them, and lock the memories in my heart and mind to treasure whenever future sunsets cross my path.

Sunset in Eleele, Hawaii

Sunset in Laugarvatn, Iceland

Acknowledgments

This book is not only about journeys, but it's also about gratitude. There are so many people I'm thankful for who have supported my journey of creating these stories and encouraged me to compile them into a book. To all, I extend heartfelt thanks.

- Jennifer Springsteen and Cleo Hehn of the former PDX Writers, where many of these stories were inspired by their creative writing prompts.
- Cleo Hehn, who now leads Creative Artists and Writers (CAW) in Portland and continues the PDX Writers legacy, along with many new spins on writing prompts. Cleo, your writing sessions always brighten my evenings!
- Claire Johnston and Andrew Zimmerman, who host the online Friday and Saturday sessions of the Power of the Pen meetup, respectively, where I've revised many of these stories and enjoyed the camaraderie of everyone who gathers there to write.
- Lyssa Orelli, my co-host of the National Alliance on Mental Illness (NAMI) Southwest Washington Creative Writing for Wellness group, and the attendees I enjoy writing with every Friday afternoon.
- Brian Benson of The Attic Institute in Portland, who introduced me to flash fiction during the peak of the COVID-19 pandemic. I was hooked after taking his beginning workshop online.
- Kathy Fish and Nancy Stohlman, who inspired me to

keep going at my first flash fiction retreat in Grand Lake, Colorado, in August 2021. They've continued their encouragement and support through their online workshops and at the fall 2023 retreat in Iceland. I'm excited about learning more from you.

- And another special thanks to Nancy Stohlman and the members of the Flash Fiction Mastermind: You mean the world to me, and I'm looking forward to continuing our writing journey together.
- HR Hegnauer, my book designer, whose talents produced a visual treat beyond my imagination.
- Susan Rooney and Eugene for letting me share the story of how they found each other.
- Last but not least, thank you to Fred Lorch, my former coworker in Massachusetts who introduced me to the Wachusett Meadow Wildlife Sanctuary, where the idea for *Rainbows in the Snow* was born.